The Woman Whisperer

- How to Naturally Strike Up Conversations • Flirt Like a Boss • And Charm Any Woman Off Her Feet •

By James Beckett

Copyright © 2016

Table of Contents

Unbroken Ice 3

Part 1: Making the Approach 6

Adjusting Your Attitude: The Mindset of the Man Who Succeeds 8

Grabbing the Moment 18

The Direct Approach 21

The Indirect Approach 25

Making an Approach When You Already Know Her 28

Part 2: Making the Right First Impression 32

    How you look 33

    The way you talk 34

    The way you hold yourself 37

    The way you treat her 41

Part 3: Jump Starting the Conversation 45

Moving On from Small Talk 50

Talking About Yourself 54

The Art of Flirting 58

The Secret of Teasing 63

Part IV: Getting That Date 67

Last Thoughts 73

Unbroken Ice

"Hi, my name is... uhh... Steve. I... um... saw you standing here and thought... well... um... hi," you stammer. She looks at you, stony faced and expectant. She's not impressed with you by the looks of it, so you're going to need to step up your game. What can you say to get her talking? You rack your brains for a sparkling piece of wit, but your mind has gone completely blank.

"So... uhhh... what's your name?" you try. She tells you in a single word, then falls silent and just keeps right on looking at you with that same unimpressed gaze. With your vague hope that she might choose to make your life a bit easier by helping you start a conversation fading fast, you begin to panic as you try to work out how to get this ice broken.

As you stand there, flustered with your mind utterly empty of good ideas, you wonder if it was such a good idea to walk over here and talk to her after all. If only the ground would swallow you up right this moment, you're sure things would be decidedly less embarrassing.

Does that sound familiar? We've all been there. You spot a woman you'd love to get to know a little better across the room, take a deep breath and steel yourself, then head on over. But once you get there, you realize pretty quickly that you aren't prepared for the task.

A cold conversation opener is never an easy thing, no matter the situation. When you add sexual attraction into the mix and the fact that both parties in this scenario are perfectly aware that you've approached her for one reason, and one reason only, it becomes even more daunting still.

I know guys who flat out refuse to approach women, purely to avoid the humiliation of this moment. I know others who avoid it at all costs because they can't bear the idea of being turned down.

But I also know plenty of guys who have mastered the art of the ice breaker and are old hands at walking up to a hot girl in a bar, saying just the right thing to snag her attention and going home that night with a phone number in their pocket.

I'm here to help you become one of those guys in the second category. It doesn't matter if you're shy or outgoing, an extravert or an introvert, good with women or just getting started. No matter who you are and what your experiences in the past have taught you, preparation here is the key to success.

It's a lot like skydiving with or without a parachute. As you stand there looking into the great, terrifying abyss, making the jump is a whole lot easier if you've prepared yourself ahead of time and made sure you have the tools to succeed right there at your fingertips.

I can understand not wanting to fling yourself into open air towards inevitable disaster because you don't have that parachute, but you're reading this book because it's the metaphorical parachute you've needed all along.

Skydiving still going to be daunting the first couple of times you try it, even with a parachute. It'll still send your insides into a spin and you'll still hesitate before you give yourself over to fate. The same goes for breaking the ice with a hot woman.

But once you have your ice breakers figured out and you know how to get the conversation started, those flutters in your stomach won't be about fear and dread of failure any more. They will be about the excitement of potential as you wonder where this conversation is going to take you.

Part 1: Making the Approach

Every romantic relationship has to start with one party approaching the other – that's simple logic. Whether it's a passionate one night affair or the start of a romance that will lead to marriage and picket fences, there's no getting around the fact that either you or she is going to need to make the first move.

If you're not equipped to break that ice, then you're left with only one option: hoping that a woman you're interested in will approach you instead. And while this is the modern world and it's much more likely she will decide to approach you than it was in the old days, you're still placing your fate entirely in somebody else's hands. Not to mention the fact that, even if she takes the plunge, you still have to impress her once the conversation gets going.

Every situation is going to be different. Perhaps you see her in a bar, chatting with her friends, and decide to approach her completely out of the blue. Maybe you find yourself waiting in line for tickets with her and decide to strike up a conversation. Maybe you are introduced to her through mutual friends, or find yourself grouped with her for a work or recreational event.

It's doesn't really matter what the exact situation is. What matters is that you understand the basic rules of approaching this woman and that you are confident in your technique as you do.

So let's start from the beginning and master the approach before we move on to the details of adding kindling to the conversation. As this is the most nerve wracking moment of all of them, it helps to feel fully confident in what you're doing.

Adjusting Your Attitude: The Mindset of the Man Who Succeeds

More than 90 percent of the communication we put out there is non verbal. In other words, how a woman evaluates you is only 10 percent to do with what you say. The rest is about your tone, your body language and your facial expressions.

It follows, therefore, that your secret weapon in approaching women is going to be your own attitude. What you want to do is exude an air of confidence and self assurance. Though you don't want to come across as cocky, you do want her to know from the outset that you have every faith in the success of your approach.

Right now, at this moment, you aren't feeling that confidence. Either you've been burned in the past attempting to approach a woman or you've never built up the nerve to even try. Whatever the case, you're certainly not feeling the tingle of potential: the telltale twist in your stomach that tells you that you're wondering about the possibilities of where this IS going to go, rather than the one that tells you you're bound to be shot down as soon as you open your mouth.

So how do you get that confidence? It's partly practice, in truth. Once you've tried out the techniques we'll be covering in this book a few times, you'll have the proof of their success that you need to feel comfortable using them.

But it's not all about practice. It's also about adjusting your attitude to become the kind of guy who has a healthy confidence in who he is and what he has to offer to that woman standing over by the bar.

Changing your mindset doesn't just change how you perceive this potential encounter and your chances of snagging her number. It also affects how you stand, how you speak, how you hold yourself and so on.

It alters everything about the non verbal communication you're putting out there. After all, how you feel affects how you think, which affects how you act. Now, instead of seeing a terrified guy who has no idea what he's doing, she sees a man who is at ease with himself and will be fun and rewarding to talk to.

Your attitude is the foundation that we'll be building everything else on top of. The stronger it is, the higher we can build the structure on top of it.

So how do you adjust your attitude to become a man who succeeds? Like this:

- **Take responsibility for everything that happens.** Everything that you achieve and everything you fail to achieve is on you and nobody else. In the past, perhaps you walked away from a failed ice breaker blaming the fact she couldn't hear you because the music was too loud, or calling her names because she wasn't interested in talking to you, or wondering if you should have worn the green shirt instead of the blue. I want you to let go of all of these excuses right now and never, ever use them again. If the ice breaker fails, it is because you did not make it succeed. You'll find that there's a strange freedom in letting go of your denials and fears. When you're prepared to accept that you are the one who makes things happen in your own life, you stop fearing the unknown and start realizing that you have control over every situation. It's up to you to make this work, which means that you have absolute opportunity to make sure it does.

- **Believe in your qualities as a dateable man.** I don't care if you look like George Clooney or the Elephant Man. I don't care if you have a Scrooge McDuck vault of pure gold or you're struggling to make the rent check every month. I don't care if you're fat or thin, short or tall, balding or sporting a thick head of hair. None of these things matter, because they don't really matter to the woman you want to talk to. Don't be fooled into thinking that women think like we do – it's not all about cheekbones and muscles for a woman, because she is only partly led by looks when she's looking for a mate. Sexual attraction for a woman is about the whole package, personality and all. Sure, your looks will factor into things, but she's also looking for a guy who presents himself well, has confidence, makes her laugh, shares her interests and will ultimately make a good life partner. The exception is, of course, a woman who is looking for a one night stand tonight with a Gerard Butler lookalike, but that really is the exception rather than the rule. Once you understand that the woman you want to approach is going to be evaluating you as a package deal, the flaws you think you have become a lot less of a worry. So what if you think your ears are too big or you're not as handsome as the dude who approached her a minute ago? What matters is the overall impression you give her, so it's time to stop sweating the small stuff.

- **Stop worrying about being shot down.** The last time you went to a restaurant, did you order everything on the menu or did you narrow your choice down to one thing? Obviously you did the latter, and you did so based on your overall tastes and what you were feeling most hungry for at that moment. Just because you didn't order the steak tips doesn't mean they are unworthy as food – you just weren't in the mood for them at that moment. Maybe when you go back next time, that's what you'll want instead. Unfortunately, far too many guys have a habit of taking a negative response from a woman completely to heart. If they approach a woman and she isn't interested, they take it as a rejection of everything about them. They forget that she might be out for a night with her friends and not looking for romance or that she might not be in the mood for a chat. They forget that a woman not being interested in them sexually doesn't mean she thinks they're an unworthy person. Nobody wants to feel that way, which is the reason so many men dread the idea of making an approach. I want you to internalize this fact before you ever even enter a bar or club: if she isn't interested, it's about HER tastes and mood and is nothing to do with who YOU are. When you understand and fully accept this fact, you can divorce yourself from the emotions of the approach just enough to able to accept that an unsuccessful attempt is not a judgment of your worth. It's just one of those things, and avoiding it really isn't worth giving up your shot at something beautiful.

- **Be your own cheerleader.** On a similar note, we all have a habit of taking other people's opinions of us more seriously than we take our own. If that hot woman doesn't find us funny, we jump to the conclusion that we are, in fact, not funny. When I put it like that, doesn't it seem a strange thing to do? It is strange, but it's only natural because human beings are wired to pick up the social cues of others to maintain our place as part of the group. Unfortunately, it's also destructive, because it's the other part of the reason we take rejection so personally. You can avoid it by becoming your own biggest fan: identify your own strengths and believe in them. I want you to write down a list of ten things about yourself that you are proud of. Hell, if you can think of twenty things, go ahead and write down twenty. Look hard at that list. Never forget what it says. Another person's opinion of you cannot change the words that are written in ink on that paper, it can only alter your perceptions of them. Keep that list handy, because I want you to look at it any time you find your faith in yourself faltering. Repeat after me: someone else's opinion of you doesn't change the truth of who you are. Be proud of that person and have confidence that you are a man who any woman would be lucky to date.

- **Put things in perspective.** Because we're all wired to procreate, we're also all wired to want to find the perfect mate. It's one of the driving forces that unites every human being on the planet and, if we're not careful, it becomes an all consuming goal. Trouble is, when you can't think of much else but finally finding the perfect woman, it shifts your attitude and in turn changes how you behave when you make the approach. Instead of seeming like a confident guy who saw a woman who sparked his interest and thought it couldn't hurt to see if she felt the same, you will appear desperate and needy. There's nothing that turns a woman off more than these things, trust me. So take a moment to remember all the things in your life that are important to you and realize that meeting women is actually only one of them. It doesn't trump your family, your career, your interests, your friends – it's only one of your life goals, not your overriding ambition. When you can put this whole adventure into that kind of perspective, it'll settle your nerves and make you more likely to be choosy and thoughtful about your approaches, which in turn will improve your success rate.

- **Forget about any woman being "out of your league".** This is such an outdated way of thinking that I don't even know where to start. Sure, the hotter the woman, the more options she has to choose from simply because the more men will express an attraction to her, but that doesn't have any bearing whatsoever on what choice she actually makes. Just because she's hot doesn't mean she's looking for a millionaire or a guy who models on the side. She's looking for exactly the same thing we all are: happiness, contentment and a soul mate she enjoys spending time with. Who's to say that doesn't describe you? There's absolutely no reason to think that it doesn't. Treat all women with exactly the same level of confidence and you might be surprised by the result.

- **If at first you fail, try and try again.** Earlier in this chapter, we talked about the idea that a woman not being interested in you is not the commentary on your looks and personality that it's so easy to take it as. There's a second part to this story. Accept right now that not every woman you approach is going to be interested in pursuing something romantic with you. We aren't attracted to every woman we see, and women aren't attracted to every man they see. Aside from not taking this personally, I want you to pinky swear that you won't let it stop you from trying the next time. Think of it like testing out flavors of ice cream until you find the one that really grabs you. You're going to approach women in abundance, because your eventual aim is to find the one that you want to call your girlfriend. Just as you probably won't discover that the first girl you approach is the one you've been waiting for all your life, you have to factor in that not every girl you approach will think the same of you. It's not a judgment, just the laws of attraction at work. Eventually – maybe on the second try, maybe on the hundredth – you're going to come across that Mrs. Right. Until you do, you have an obligation to your own happiness to keep on trying.

Grabbing the Moment

There's a golden moment when a man and a woman enter the same physical space. That golden moment is the one in which you can approach her, initiate conversation and maybe, just maybe, walk out of there with the promise of a date.

One of the biggest problems guys face when it comes to approaching women is the tendency to miss this golden moment. Maybe you're sat near her in a coffee shop and, because you hesitated, she leaves. Maybe you wait too long in a bar and another dude walks up to her instead.

Maybe you see her at the gym and, because you waited, she got stuck into her routine and you don't feel like you can interrupt her. Maybe she was lined up in front of you at the supermarket and, because you hesitated, you had to pay for your groceries as she walked out the door.

Missing that golden moment is tantamount to giving up on approaching a woman entirely. To be successful, you need to be in a state of mind where you see her, realize you'd like to talk to her and immediately do it, before the moment has passed.

What usually makes guys miss that golden moment? Fear. It's fear of all the things we talked about in that last chapter: rejection, uncertainty or even just not knowing what to say. Trust me that, by the end of this book, you'll know exactly what to say. In the last chapter, we also worked on your mindset to help you develop the confidence to make those approaches.

So, for you, there will be nothing actually standing in the way of making your approach. The only thing that's going to stop you is your own mind and the defense mechanisms it has in place to avoid the risk of emotional trauma.

You will stop yourself because you are weighing up the risks versus the potential rewards. Your internal monologue is going to tell you to slow down a moment and think about what it will mean if she rejects you, demanding that you gather more information so you can determine how likely it is that will happen.

What your mind is really doing is trying to talk you out of it because your subconscious is doing its best to look out for you and make sure you don't put yourself in a situation where you could get hurt. It's the same thing as fearing heights or spiders – your mind elicits a reaction from you that's unpleasant and therefore stops you from stepping off the edge of a cliff or walking into a web.

Making you hesitate is another way of stopping you from hurting yourself, only, in this case, it's about protecting you from emotional pain. Because all of this is happening over the space of minutes – or maybe even seconds – your subconscious is using delay tactics to protect you from that possible rejection.

The only way past this problem is to have made the decision already. Tell yourself right now, in this moment, that you will never hesitate to approach a woman you find alluring. Tell yourself that you accept there is a risk she won't be interested, but that you know that what could happen if she does find you attractive far outweighs that possibility.

Tell yourself this now and you won't need to cover the same ground when the opportunity does arise. Rather than listen to your subconscious and miss your golden moment, you'll be able to dismiss its delay tactics because you recognize them for what they are. You'll be able to take the plunge and approach that woman while the moment is right.

The Direct Approach

There are two main ways you can approach a woman. The first way is to strike up a conversation without ever mentioning your interest in her and then seeing where it goes. The other way is the one we're going to look at first.

The direct approach is riskier and rejection will come much more quickly, if it's going to come. That makes it much, much scarier, especially for a beginner. Worry not: if you don't feel you're up to the challenge quite yet, you can build up to using a direct approach. We'll look at the easier method in the next chapter.

So why would you want to use the direct approach? Well, lots of reasons.

- It lays out your intentions fast, so you don't waste any time dithering around the point and then find out after three hours of chatting that she has a fiancé.

- It shows her that you are confident and bold, creating a positive first impression.

- It will trigger a response from her immediately, making her think about you from the outset as a possible mate.

- It's often the only way to go about approaching a woman if you have only a short time window to speak with her. For instance, if you're sat next to her on a train or if you pass her on the street.

- Many women will appreciate your honesty and prefer that you make yourself clear rather than beat about the bush for hours before you state your attraction to her.

- For you, it can feel more natural and less like you're playing a game with this woman, which can in turn make you feel and act more comfortably.

Approaching a woman directly is pretty straightforward. If you choose this method, you will quite literally walk up to her, introduce yourself and let her know that you find her attractive. It helps to have identified exactly what it is that makes you feel attracted to her, too, to make the approach more personal and instantly let her know that you've noticed her for a legitimate reason.

Depending on the situation, you might then ask her if you could buy her a drink, join her where she's sitting, meet her for a coffee later or whatever else applies. You're not asking her on a date quite yet; what you are suggesting is that, in a casual setting that doesn't require either of you to commit to anything, you take the chance to get to know each other better and see if that attraction is mutual.

It really is as simple as that. A few examples to illustrate what I mean:

- "Hi there, I'm Jacob. I saw you from across the room and couldn't help but notice how beautiful you are. Would you mind if I joined you for a little while?"

- "Hi, I'm Mathew. You look absolutely stunning this evening and I find your eyes so hypnotizing – I was hoping you might allow me to buy you a drink?"

- "Hello, my name is John. I can't help but be intrigued by what you're doing, I'm a big fan of fantasy football too. May I sit with you? I'd like to get to know you better."

- "Hi, I'm Curt. I can see you're busy right now but I haven't been able to tear my eyes from you and I'd like to buy you a coffee when you have time."

What these approaches all have in common is that they state your interest right off the bat BUT then put the ball in the woman's court. You aren't forcing her to put up with your presence if she doesn't want to. You aren't making any assumptions about whether or not she'd like to get to know you.

Instead, you are offering her an opportunity and it's up to her whether she takes it. A bold, direct approach can be extremely successful, but only if she feels she has a choice in the matter. If you force your presence on her, she's going to reject you purely because you made her feel uncomfortable.

If your approach is successful, she will agree to spend some time with you. The approach has worked and you can now move on to breaking the ice. We'll cover what you should do next in the section after this one.

The Indirect Approach

The opposite of direct is, of course, indirect, and this style of approach tends to be easier for beginners and those of us who feel too shy to just blurt out our feelings from the get go.

It also has its own advantages. It allows the woman a little time to form an impression of you before she is forced to make up her mind as to whether she is attracted to you. As attraction for the fairer sex is a package deal, this can work in your favor – and it can boost your confidence in your success if you're still worried that you don't look like a movie star.

In some scenarios, it's also a much better idea than to be direct. If a woman is in a situation where she feels at all vulnerable, such as if she's alone on the street at night or in a testosterone heavy environment, she will be understandably on edge about her safety. The direct approach, in this case, may trigger her to feel uncertainty or even fear.

The indirect approach can also actually be more effective, depending on her personality. While some women will appreciate directness, others will appreciate that you gave them the time and space to make up their minds before you posed the question of whether they find you attractive.

Again, the biggest factor in this style of approach is that you make sure to seize your moment while it is fresh. Bite the bullet and walk up to her with a smile on your face.

Then, you can initiate a conversation that is non threatening and, hopefully, piques her interest. For instance:

- Make an observation about the place you are both in, such as, "I'd say this place isn't worth the wait at the bar if it wasn't for their Moscow Mules".

- Ask her a question that focuses on your shared experience of the place you're both in right now, such as, "Hey, have you tried the sauna room here?"

- Ask her a question that focuses on something about her specifically, showing that you've paid some attention to who she is and what she's doing before you approached, such as, "I see you're reading *The Fault in Our Stars.* I heard it was much better than the movie, are you finding that to be true?"

Questions – or statements that provoke an answer – are always your best tactic in this situation because they give her an obvious way to continue the conversation if she wants to. Once you've sparked that conversation, you can continue it for as long as you feel necessary to put both of you at ease before suggesting that you maybe take her for a drink or a coffee, or go find a table so you can get to know each other better.

Making an Approach When You Already Know Her

The rules change when you approach a woman who you already know in some capacity. Turning an acquaintanceship into something more is actually the easiest of all approaches, partly because it's less nerve wracking for you and partly because your chances of success are substantially higher.

In this scenario, you've spoken with this woman before. Maybe you go to the same gym or you work on the same floor. Maybe you run into her regularly at your favorite bar or you've met her a couple of times through a mutual friend.

However you met her those first few times doesn't matter. What's important is that you've made the decision that you are attracted to her and would like to make an approach – and that you've already cracked the ice at least part of the way.

You already have a connection with her, even if it's a tenuous one. This is hugely important because it means she already has a certain level of comfort with you, because you are already a familiar face.

This allows you to bypass the biggest and most common problem in approaching women: her uncertainty of your intentions and whether she can trust you. We are all wary of strangers – that's how we keep ourselves away from danger – but, for women, it's a more exaggerated feeling than for men.

The reason for that is obvious: her personal safety. The truth of the matter is that men are bigger, stronger and therefore more dangerous to women than vice versa. She knows at her core that she must always protect herself and thus will hesitate to immediately trust a new face.

When you've already made it past this barrier, you'll find that she's much more willing to give your approach her consideration. She may not trust you completely, but she knows from experience that you have not done her harm during your previous encounters and so will be more open to developing that trust.

When you approach her, you'll also find it much easier to strike up a conversation because you can base it around that common ground. You can ask her how her latest gym session went, or ask if she's seen your mutual friend recently. You need only continue the small talk for a short while to re-establish those comfort levels and give her time to get used to speaking with you.

Once your intuition is telling you that the ice has been broken, let her know your intentions. You're not pausing in the street to acknowledge an acquaintance here, you're approaching this woman in the hopes of securing a date.

So, tell her so. At that golden moment in the conversation when your gut is telling you it's right, tell her you were hoping she'd let you take her out for dinner or a drink, or that she'd join you for a coffee before she goes home. If the attraction is mutual, your success is all but guaranteed.

As you can see, the familiarity factor can be your biggest ally in an approach. It's so much easier to strike up a conversation with someone you already know, even if you are strongly attracted to them and nervous of whether or not they feel the same. It's so much easier for her to let down her guard and give you the positive response you are hoping for, too.

If you're thinking to yourself, "Well, that's all very well, but I don't have any acquaintances I'm attracted to," there's a simple solution to that, as well. Go and find some.

Broaden your horizons beyond the bar and the club and start enjoying some activities that are naturally social. Join a class, take up a hobby, become part of a club or society. Take up a new sport, volunteer for a charity group, accept invitations to your friends' parties and social gatherings.

All of these activities will give you the chance to meet new people – and some of these new people are bound to be worth considering as possible dates. Not only will you enrich your life in ways you weren't expecting, you'll also be spending more time around people and you'll be much more likely to come into contact with a woman you'd just love to spend some one-on-one time with.

So get on out there and spread your social wings. After all, you don't have to wait for opportunity to come knocking. You can get out there right now and find that opportunity for yourself.

Part 2: Making the Right First Impression

Let's pause for a moment to think about what this hot woman is thinking as you approach her. As we mentioned already, she is going to start sizing you up from the very instant that you initiate contact with her, whether she's met you in the past or you're a completely new puzzle.

As soon as she becomes aware that you are a potential suitor, she's going to begin forming an impression of you and deciding whether you are the type of guy she would like to know better – and whether you're the type of guy she might be interested in sexually and romantically.

The perfect opening line is not going to be enough to solidify this first impression. Sure, it's vital to get it right so that you can get the process rolling, but it's only one small part of what's going to go through her mind.

Remember how we discussed that talking to a woman is only ten percent about what you say and 90 percent about your body language, attitude and tone? The impression she forms of you is going to come from HOW you speak to her, as well as from what you say.

It'll come from the way you're dressed, your facial expressions, how you hold yourself, your movements and so on. So let's make sure we get that part of things right.

How? By making sure you are paying attention to every signal you're giving her. To do that, make sure you're paying attention to:

How you look
I'm not suggesting a facelift here, I'm recommending that you make sure at all times (and particularly when you're going out with the specific intention of meeting women) that you are presenting yourself in the best light.

Whittle down your wardrobe to only the outfits that flatter you, are smart and clean and are free from stains or blemishes. It doesn't matter whether it's a three piece suit or a band tshirt and jeans, you want to look as though you pay attention to your personal hygiene and take pride in your appearance.

This also goes for your body: make sure you are freshly showered, you've paid attention to your hair and facial hair and you smell good. Believe me when I tell you that, while preferences will vary wildly as to whether a woman prefers a turtle neck and slacks or the goth look, all women prefer a man who is well groomed and well put together.

A man who has an egg stain and holes in his faded tshirt and looks like he hasn't taken a bath in at least a month is telling a woman, "I look this bad when I'm trying to make a good impression on you, so you can bet your ass that I'm the kind of life partner who'll be a smelly lump on the sofa asking you to bring me another beer from the fridge all day long". Not attractive and not the type of guy she's looking to invite into her life.

A man who is clean, wearing interesting clothes and obviously takes care of himself, on the other hand, is more likely to be the kind of man who is reliable, thoughtful and able to take care of his own business.

The way you talk

There are so many common mistakes that guys make when they start talking to a woman, most of them due to pure nervousness. It's important that you regulate your speech during this first encounter and make absolutely sure you're following these rules:

- **Slow down your voice.** It's all too easy to blurt out your words as quickly as you possibly can, worried that she'll cut you off or get bored before you finish unless you hurry things along. When you speak that quickly, you make it obvious that you feel nervous. Either that, or you might be high. Either way, it's going to convey a sense of discomfort to her because she will pick up on your nervousness. Instead, keep your voice slow and steady, pause where you would normally pause. Keep in mind that the kind of male voices most commonly called "most sexy" are slow, low drawls. Slow your voice down as much as you possibly can without sounding like a robot – you'll seem relaxed, more confident and genuinely sexier.

- **Keep a smile on your face.** You'll be surprised how much this affects the tone of your voice. You don't have to grin at her like a lunatic, but keep at least the hint of a smile during the beginnings of the conversation. Have you ever spoken to someone on the phone and felt sure they were smiling on the other end? That's because we humans are so very good at detecting body language that we can literally hear a smile in a person's tone. It makes us feel comfortable and it makes us want to smile in return, and that's exactly what you want her to be feeling right now.

- **Lower your voice.** Again, this is an impression that will be entirely unconscious on her part, but that doesn't mean it won't affect her thinking. A lower voice is perceived as more manly because it implies more testosterone in your body. When we get nervous, it tends to affect the pitch of our voice and so, when you approach a woman, it's natural that your voice will be higher than usual. Physically speaking, this is because you will be tensed up and you'll speak from your throat, which is easier to achieve in that situation. Take a deep breath, relax and speak from your stomach, which will lower your pitch to a more normal depth and in turn seem much sexier and more masculine.

- **Project your voice.** Another common side effect of feeling nervous is that feeling of wanting to hide. It comes across in your voice very strongly, because you'll unconsciously try to "hide" your voice by speaking more quietly than you usually would. This can easily turn into a mumble or a mutter that the woman you're speaking to can barely even hear. It's not fun to constantly ask someone to repeat themselves and it makes us feel uncomfortable if we're not quite sure we heard someone right.

After a while, it gets pretty annoying. Make sure you are speaking at your regular volume, you are enunciating your words and that your head is tilted towards her, rather than down, so that you are projecting your words clearly in her direction. She'll find it much easier to settle into a conversation with you if she doesn't feel concerned about actually hearing you.

The way you hold yourself
Your body will be telling her a whole lot about who you are, even if you're not paying any attention to it. Imagine, if you will, a guy who is looking at the floor and fiddling with his hands, slouched over and turned slightly away from you. Compare that to a guy who is standing up straight and still while looking you in the eye, only using gestures when they will punctuate what he is saying.

Which of these two gentleman would you prefer to speak with? The first dude seems uncomfortable and nervous and doesn't really give the impression of someone who wants to be in the same room as you, let alone someone who is going to be a thrilling conversationalist. The second guy? Well, he's not giving off any signals that would make you second guess whether you want to talk to him.

- **Adopt a good posture.** Straighten your back and stand with your legs slightly parted, knees not locked. Put your arms somewhere they feel natural, such as hooked into your pockets or holding a bottle of beer. Your posture should feel natural rather than forced, but it is also important that it projects self confidence and comfort.

- **Look her in the eye.** I cannot stress strongly enough how important eye contact is at this moment. If you let your eyes stray away too much or even start darting around the room, you give the impression of feeling guilty or being dishonest. She'll pick up on that quickly, believe me. On the other hand, eye contact is one of the fundamental building blocks when it comes to new relationships. Something about maintaining another person's gaze makes us feel connected to them and starts the synapses in our brains zapping back and forth with the kind of chemicals that make us feel attached to another person. Try not to stare at her with bug eyes, which is just as disconcerting as not looking at her at all, and do make sure to temporarily break contact every so often, when it feels natural, so that you relieve some of the building pressure you're creating with your gaze. But most of the time while you're talking to her, you will find that looking her right in the eye helps to create exactly the bond you are looking for.

- **Keep your smile handy.** We already talked about making sure you have a smile on your face during your opener because she will hear it in the tone of your voice, but smiling in general is a crucial part of your body language when approaching a woman. Our minds are wired to mimic the emotions of the person we are speaking with – that's why watching a character in a movie cry makes you feel sad too. When you smile at her, it will make her feel like smiling back. It's also a signal of good intentions, no matter the situation, so a smile will increase her comfort levels at the same time. Of course, if you grin inanely with wide eyes and all your teeth bared, she's going to think you're a lunatic. Aim for a half smile and make sure you mean it, because we humans can also tell the difference between a "real" smile that reaches the person's eyes and a "fake" smile that only affects what the mouth is doing. Flash her a big grin when one of you makes a joke and feel free to be generous with your laugh but, when talking normally, stick to a gentle smile that's reassuring and evokes a smile from her in return. The caveat to this is, of course, that you shouldn't grin like a maniac if the conversation turns to more serious matters. You're safe to let your smile drop when the conversation gets deeper and more involved, though it's a good idea to pepper in some lighter moments wherever possible so you can bring that smile back in.

- **Tone down your gestures.** A person who communicates largely through arm movements and gestures either appears to be nervous and unconfident, or not that bright. We have a tendency to interpret liberal use of gestures to mean that the person who is using them simply lacks the vocabulary to communicate their ideas with words, which in turn makes us assume they are unintelligent or uneducated. While that's not actually always true, it's a risk you don't want to take when you're trying to make a first impression. Nervousness also makes us more jittery and uncoordinated, which will make your gestures more awkward and disconcerting to watch.

Keep your arms in the position you placed them when setting your posture and reserve your gestures for when you tell a particularly good story or make a joke, when they will punctuate your words in a positive way.

The way you treat her
It's never too early to start showing her how much of a gentleman you are. Even in those very first moments of speaking with her, you can either be giving her the impression that you don't much care about what she's thinking and feeling, or you could be showing her that you are attentive and thoughtful of her needs.

There are two main ways you can do this. The first is to make sure that you are genuinely and obviously more interested in her than you are in bogarting the conversation. Most of us make the mistake at least once in our lives of making a conversation all about ourselves. Sometimes it's because we're nervous, sometimes we like someone so much that we subconsciously want to tell them everything there is to know about ourselves as fast as possible to seal the deal. Sometimes it's just bad manners.

If you want her to feel that you are interested in her as a person and genuinely want to get to know her better, then the best way to do that is to prove it. Ask her questions about herself and then ask follow up questions to make it clear you were listening and you really do want to know more about her. Listen to her carefully without interrupting.

Above all else, don't ask her a question as an excuse to tell her something about you. For instance, don't ask her if she's ever traveled abroad just so you can say, "Oh really? Well I've been to India and Germany and Nepal and Ireland and..."

If you're lucky enough to find yourself talking about deep and meaningful topics during this first encounter, make sure you make the most of the opportunity. If she tells you her views and opinions on politics or social rights, for instance, encourage her to open up more rather than seizing the opportunity to challenge her and be "right".

The second way to give her the right impression of your manners is to quite literally have good manners. Pay attention to her and her needs – open doors, offer to refresh her drink, be polite to her friends if they come over to join the conversation and so on. This shows her that you have respect for her and her comfort, which she will appreciate on a deep level.

One last thing while you're doing all this: be sure to keep an eye on her reactions. Just as you're giving a strong impression of who you are and what you are feeling through your body language, you will be able to tell a lot about this woman through her own.

Ideally, she will have a smile on her face and will seem relaxed and happy to make eye contact with you. She will be relatively close to you and leaning in towards you.

If any of this changes, take it as an immediate alert. If she isn't smiling in tune with you, if she has her arms folded or starts to seem tense, if she backs away from you or turns all or part of her body away from yours, she is telling you that she is not comfortable in the conversation.

If this happens, quickly take stock of the situation. Have you said something wrong or moved too quickly? Was she doing this from the start, suggesting she might not really want to speak to you?

You can try backing off a little, changing the topic and making sure you've got your body language bases covered. Particularly if her body language has only just begun to change, this can solve the problem fairly quickly. If it doesn't work, you might be best to politely end the conversation and walk away, which is what she is trying to signal that she wants you to do.

That's going to be difficult for you to do, I know. You wanted to meet this woman and get to know her and you don't want to give up your chance quite yet. But if you don't see any signs that lightening the conversation or fixing your body language is working, it's unlikely you're going to get a positive result.

Best to break the link right now – if she was just feeling overwhelmed, who knows? Maybe you'll get another chance to make your impression later.

Part 3: Jump Starting the Conversation

Here we are at the moment of truth – the moment, if you're honest, that I know you've been dreading. Whether you choose to go direct or indirect, you will need fairly early on in this process to be able to get a conversation going. If you choose the indirect route, you'll be doing this right away.

If you choose the direct approach, you'll hopefully be finding yourself a quiet corner or choosing a booth at the cafe and facing each other for a chat. Though you started the adventure by boldly stating you were attracted to her, you can't spend the next hour repeating that statement – you still need to initiate some sort of conversation.

This, for most guys, is the hardest moment of all. It's the moment when your brain goes blank and every fact you ever knew comes flying out of your ears. The pressure is on and your mind instantly starts working against you.

Fortunately, that's much less likely to happen when you have prepared ahead of time. When you know how to go about starting a conversation, all you need to do is follow your own step by step rules and you'll know exactly what to do.

So, when you find yourself approaching a hot woman, I want you to ask yourself three questions:

1. **Where are we?** The environment you are in may provide you with some clues about her interests and who she is. It may also allow you to formulate an interesting observation about the place – remember, both you and she have chosen to be here and do whatever activity is associated with this place, so you have some common ground simply through shared vicinity.

2. **What is she doing?** It can really help you out to spend just a few moments evaluating what she is doing and why. Is she dancing at the club? Is she reading a book or magazine? What is she paying attention to – a screen, a performer? Is she carrying or wearing something interesting? Identify something about her that sets her apart from everyone else in the immediate vicinity and simply ask her about it.

3. **What impressions of her have I gathered already?** Even a cursory glance at another human being usually gives us an impression of

what they are like. Sometimes that impression can be misleading, but most of the time it gives us enough data to go on to make an initial evaluation of who they are and what they are like. Let's say she's with a group of friends and they are hanging on her every word, laughing like crazy at everything she says. That would give you a distinctly different impression than if she was sat alone at a table in a restaurant with papers spread around her and a laptop, her brow furrowed in concentration. You can use this evaluation to help gauge what sort of a conversation she might be interested in. The belle of the ball may prefer a joke, or a silly question such as, "I was wondering, if you could have any super power, which would you choose?" The woman who is focused and driven may prefer that you find a more meaningful topic to discuss, such as current affairs.

Use these questions to make a quick decision about exactly what you want to say when you approach her. It's always best to do this before you actually walk up to her and open your mouth because, as with most things in life, the unknown is a lot less terrifying when we feel we're prepared for it.

Once you've evaluated these things, you have one last task ahead of you before you can settle in. You need to ask her, "So, what are you up to right now?"

You need to ask this because it will give you a reasonable idea of how long you're going to have to make your impression on her. If she's heading to work or an event, you may only have a couple of minutes to shine. If she's doing something shortly but isn't in a hurry, you'll have five, maybe ten minutes to break the ice. But if she's not doing much at all right now, you'll theoretically have as long as you need.

In the first scenario, you'll need to be direct with her pretty quickly. You can fit in maybe one question and answer, preferably something that makes her laugh, before you'll need to ask for her number.

In the second scenario, you can evolve the conversation a little bit further, but not a whole lot, so you should still try to make her smile and laugh and give a good impression of yourself quickly, but then you'll need to move on to asking for her number.

In the third scenario, you can relax and just keep right on chatting until your gut is telling you it's time to ask if you can see her again. I recommend choosing a moment where both of you are relaxed, making eye contact and laughing together.

So let's move on to conversational tactics. With all of them in your repertoire, you'll be able to choose the right one on the spur of the moment and switch between them at ease during the time you have to spend with her, whether it's 30 seconds or the rest of your evening.

Moving On from Small Talk

Whichever else of the techniques we're about to cover you master, this one is the bedrock of your success in approaching women. It's imperative that you never forget to make a connection with a woman you're interested in and that you do it as quickly and thoroughly as you can.

You'll start with small talk, or a silly question, or a discussion about where you are and what you're doing. That's always a good way to get her smiling and get through the initial couple of minutes while she's evaluating her own safety, but now you want to build a rapport.

The reason you want to do this is threefold. First, it's because we feel closer to people we've talked to about ourselves and more inclined to trust and like them. Second, because small talk does very little to spark her emotions – but sharing personal information definitely will. Third, because your interest in her will flatter her ego and will make her perceive her time with you as much more interesting.

So here's what you're going to do: ASK QUESTIONS. I capitalized that so it would jump out at you and attach itself to your brain.

You need to get her to open up about herself, so you need to show some interest in who she is and what she does with her life.

Now, you need to be careful how you structure those questions. You don't want to ask her too many questions that can be answered in a single word or sentence, because then it turns into the kind of atmosphere you'd find in a courtroom. In a lot of cases, you'll find that "getting to know you" questions do fall into that category, so the secret of success here is always be ready with a follow up.

I'm going to give you some examples. Each one will have at least two questions; the first one, maybe even two, will evoke a short answer from her, the second and sometimes third will open up the conversation much more widely.

- "So do you live around here?" "How did you end up moving to the city?"

- "Where are you from originally?" "What was it like there?"

- "What do you do for a living?" "That's cool — what made you decide you wanted to do that?"

- "Where did you go to school?" "What did you study?" "What made you choose to study that?" "What did you enjoy most about it?"

- "Do you go to gigs like this often?" "What's your favorite kind of music?" "How did you get into it?" "What's the coolest gig you've ever been to?"

Now, I'm not suggesting that you write down a list of questions and then work your way through them. What I am suggesting is that you ask her questions about as many aspects of her life as possible and that you are always ready with a follow up question to keep her talking.

You'll need to do this more while the encounter is still feeling a little awkward but, as time goes on and she begins to open up more, her answers will get longer. When this happens, you can shift your focus slightly.

If you're listening carefully to her answers – and you'd better be, because there's nothing more off putting than not being listened to – you'll be able to pick up on small details of her stories and ask her more about them.

For instance, let's say you ask her if she likes to travel and follow up by asking her about her most interesting trip overseas. She starts telling you about her visit to South America and talks about the sights she saw there. You can ask her more about the sights themselves, whether she got to see something in particular, which one she thought was the most impressive, whether any of them stick in her memory as being particularly meaningful and so on.

Questions are incredibly powerful during a first conversation because they make it easy for her to keep talking to you without any of those awkward pauses that make first dates so excruciating. Being a good listener is also one of those wonderful qualities that we're all looking for in a partner, so you'll also be giving her an excellent impression of who you are.

So sit back, relax and listen to her and be ready with your next follow up question when she finishes her stories. You might be surprised at just how far that's going to get you.

Talking About Yourself

While you don't want to dominate the conversation and come across as the kind of guy who is far too self interested to care what she thinks, you do want to share a few things about yourself along the way. By the time you part ways, you want her to feel like she knows you better, even if you barely shared anything at all.

It's a delicate balance, but a necessary one. If you are still a blank slate, how does she know whether she's interested enough to give you her phone number? But if you've detailed your whole life history, why would she think you were anything other than self centered?

The key here is to consider those moments when you talk about yourself as extended questions. In other words, you are only really talking about yourself to spark her interest in a new topic and get her talking about her own thoughts and feelings again. You are going to yield the floor to her as quickly as you can, as soon as you've given her something about yourself to chew on.

You are going to do this even if she's an excellent conversationalist herself and is doing her best to open you up and get you talking. By all means answer her questions in as much detail as is needed (because you don't want to seem as though you're evading her questions), but don't be afraid to end by asking for the same information in return.

So what about yourself should you reveal? The most important qualities that you have to offer her. Maybe you're adventurous, kind, ambitious, sociable and thoughtful. You want to tell her stories that will get this qualities across.

So let's say she asks what you do for a living. You're not going to give her a single sentence as an answer, you're going to weave a story for her, because that's much more captivating for her as an audience. You're going to include the answer you would have given to a follow up question, too. For instance:

"I'm actually training to be a nurse right now. I was working in construction for a while but it just wasn't fulfilling me and I couldn't work out why. Then it finally hit me that the one thing I did like about what I was doing was seeing people move into the houses I built – I liked thinking about how happy they would be with the extra details we put in the bathroom and how carefully we thought about the kitchen layout. I realized I like helping people and making them happy, so I figured it was time to switch directions and do something that would really make me come home each day feeling like I'd done some good. So how about you, what made you decide to become a teacher?"

Analyze that example for a moment. The key aspects of it are:

- It's a story, so it's immediately more interesting than hearing bare facts.

- It's honest and detailed, so she feels like she got a glimpse into your mind.

- It highlights positive qualities about you: you like to help people and you have enough insight into yourself to be able to make that career change.

- It switches the conversation back to her as soon as you're finished. Rather than let things trail off, you've turned your focus back onto getting to know her.

We all have interesting reasons for why we picked our careers, why we enjoy certain hobbies, why we like some music, food and movies more than others. Maybe you like cooking because your mother was a chef who used to invite you into the kitchen to test out new recipes with her. Maybe you like reading because you're a sponge for new information and you can't help but want to learn more new things every day. Maybe you chose law at school but part way through your second year you realized that you hated every moment and decided to be a florist instead. Tell her these stories and then ask for her own in return.

The more interesting, intriguing and entertaining your stories are, the better. When it's your turn to speak, you can tell her amusing anecdotes about moments in your life and you can give her insight into what makes you tick. By doing that, you will pique her interest in finding out more and you'll give her the insight into you that she needs to decide whether she wants to give you a chance on a date.

The Art of Flirting

You're having this conversation because you are attracted to this woman, right? You approached her because you want to get to know her better and you'd love for that connection to turn into something more.

It follows, therefore, that you want this to be clear throughout your time together. You want there to be a burning sexual tension that both of you are eager to explore further. It's that tension that will make her agree to go on a date with you.

But you don't want to scare her away by being over the top sexual at her – no woman wants to feel like a guy is metaphorically shaking his junk in her face. You want a subtle thread of flirting to run through your whole encounter, slowly building on its own without ever bubbling to the surface.

By flirting gently and innocently, you make your intentions clear without pushing too hard and making her feel uncomfortable. It's a subtle art that takes practice, but first of all you're going to need to overcome the two dangerous mistakes that guys tend to make when they're flirting with women:

- Don't be blunt. The best flirts in the world know that subtlety is key and that a woman will be much more excited by suggestions and hints that leave a little mystery for them to uncover.

- Don't be sexual. It's off putting at the best of times and will kill your chances of getting her number every time. You don't want to make any overt sexual comments about how she looks or what you'd like to do to her.

Fortunately, most of the flirting you'll be doing is going to require no words at all – it's all about how you act and how you hold yourself.

When you flirt without words, you see, you can convey your true feelings for her without ever stepping over the line into freaking her out. Here's how you can turn up the heat while you're getting to know her during that first conversation:

- Make sure to hold that eye contact, but let your eyes move every so often to her lips.

- Let your eyes relax as you look at her just enough so that you are neither staring at her nor looking like you're about to doze off. These are the "bedroom eyes" she'll find tough to resist.

- Move a little closer to her as the conversation moves on. Physical proximity has an impact on our emotions and make us feel intimate with a person.

- Lean towards her and make sure that your body is pointing towards hers, giving her your full attention.

- Touch her every so often at the base of her back, on her elbow and at the top of her arm. Touch is incredibly powerful in building a rapport with another person and a gentle caress in a flirting situation can send pleasure zapping from her skin to her brain.

- Find reasons to touch her – ask to see her bracelet or look closer at her ring, for instance. Don't do this too often, but every so often it can be an excellent cherry on the flirting cake.

- Slow down your voice and lower your tone.

- Lean in and speak directly in her ear when the music or the crowd gets loud. Don't stay there too long or she'll start to feel crowded – just long enough for her to tingle at how close you are.

- Mimic her body language. When she tilts her head to one side, for example, you should do the same.

Using your body, you've successfully set the stage. You've made it clear you're interested in her and, subconsciously, she's now well aware that this conversation has a deeper meaning than just a casual chat between two people who just met.

While you're doing this, you're also going to invoke the most successful flirting style of all: the witty flirt. Make her laugh while you're flirting with her and you can get away with some pretty outrageous comments.

You can be cheesy, silly or simply over exaggerate – tell her she's obviously talking to you so she can make her move but you're an innocent who mustn't be taken advantage of. Ask her if she works out and, when she returns the question, say, "Not usually, but I popped out and lifted weights for an hour before I came to talk to you, just in case you're into that kind of thing."

You can even tell lies in the name of making her laugh. If she accuses you playfully of telling all the girls they have pretty eyes, make her grin by saying, "You heard about that? Darn, I must not be as subtle as I thought". If she asks what you do for a living, tell her you're a championship wrestler but she mustn't tell anyone as you're here incognito.

Keep up the flirting throughout the conversation, stepping it up and down throughout so that it's a constant presence without preventing you from holding a conversation that lets you get to know each other better. Think of it as the spice in the cake mix – it's what's going to turn your approach from a getting to know you interview into the promise of something more.

The Secret of Teasing

Teasing is another one of those tricky skills that is going to require your judgment and some practice to get right. If you get it wrong, there is a possibility you may upset or offend her or even hurt her feelings, none of which is going to get you any closer to a date with her.

But if you find the right balance and manage to tease her with the barb taken out of your stinger, you will make her laugh and actually send her subtle signals that you like her very much, even when your words are saying you don't.

Teasing is also a skill that goes hand in hand with flirting and produces very similar results. For that reason, if you're not entirely sure how she might react to being teased, you can always play it safe and go with simple flirting instead. On the other hand, if the flirting is going great, you can use teasing to ramp up the tempo and really start that connection between the two of you buzzing.

The secret of successful teasing is as follows: you should always choose topics to tease her about that are things you actually LIKE about her, or that she likes about herself.

Never mock her for her looks or how she dresses, nor for any of the values she holds important. Don't imply she's stupid or take the mickey out of her friends – these are things that will either make her defensive or could actually be a blow to her self esteem.

You'll find "dating guides" out there that encourage you to do exactly that on the basis that it makes you a challenge she wants to overcome, but I highly recommend ignoring that advice. It might work on some women, but it's not going to be your best approach even then – and, if it goes wrong, it will drive her away quicker than you can say, "I'm sorry, I do think your hair is really pretty".

So when you're looking for something to tease about her, think about the things that make her unique – the reasons you're still stood next to her, having this conversation.

Let's say she has this really cute habit of twisting her hair around her finger. "Careful, you're gonna snap that off," you could say with a grin. She'll smile, but she'll also know that you've been paying enough attention to her to see her little quirks.

Maybe she's wearing a really unusual, really big ring. "I'm kinda hoping that guy over there tries to hit on you, I want to see how much damage that thing does when you punch him," you could say.

You can also teasingly accuse her of flirting with you. Both of you know that you're actually signaling your interest in HER, but you're doing it in a non threatening way. "Did you just check out my butt?" is always a good one, as it will make her squeal a denial. "I know why you're buying me this drink. It's because you think you can seduce me, isn't it? Well, I'm a good boy, I can see through your wiles lady," is another good one.

You can also use stereotypes, as long as you make it obvious you don't really mean it. She's from Kentucky? "Hey cool, did you bring any chicken?" might work. She's a psychology major? "So are you reading my mind right now?" will make her roll her eyes and grin.

As you tease her, keep a watchful eye on her reaction. For most women, you'll see her eyes light up and sparkle in amusement when you tease her. If you don't, it might not be something she responds to all that well, so take a step back and try something else.

But if she is responding well, you'll probably start to see more physical interaction from her too, as she swats you playfully or pretends to push you away.

These are great things as they will literally bring you closer and get things heating up fast between the two of you.

Part IV: Getting That Date

Here we are at the final stage. You've swallowed your nervousness and approached this woman, you've started a conversation with her and you've been chatting for long enough now that you instinctively know there's a connection between you.

You're still very much interested in getting to know her on a more intimate level and you can sense that she also is liking what she sees. Maybe your time together is coming to an end – the bar is closing, the party is over, her train is coming down the track. Maybe you simply feel like cutting things off now will leave her wanting more, which will make her more likely to want to see you again.

If the latter is the case, you should definitely go with that instinct. There comes a moment in every first conversation where the obvious topics have been covered and you've connected just enough that you could easily slip into the kind of long conversation that will last all night. It's not necessarily a bad idea to give in to that temptation, but you can also choose to leave that chat for your first official date.

But, at the end of the day, it doesn't really matter WHY you've reached the point where you want to ask her if she'll meet up with you again. It just matters that you're there and that you have one more bullet to bite before you're done.

Even though you've come this far and she's encouraged you every step of the way, it's not uncommon to feel seriously nervous at this moment. I know that, you know that, and we both also know that it's vital you don't let fear overwhelm you.

Don't let all that hard work go to waste – make sure you lock her in for a follow up and you get the opportunity you've wanted since the start to go on a date with her.

The best way to quell those fears is to remember this: you're not asking her to marry you. You're not even asking her to be your girlfriend. You're just asking her if she would like to carry on this conversation at a later time.

It's just a date, no more and no less. Your chances of her saying yes are also sky high right now, while she's still smiling and feeling all those good, positive emotions from the time you've spent together.

So let's go for it, shall we? As soon as you find an appropriate moment, let's ask her if she'd like to meet you again on a date.

Before you say anything out loud, I want you to think back on everything you've discovered about her over the course of the conversation. What music does she like? What's her favorite food? Where does she generally hang out in the evenings? Does she enjoy sports? The theater? What are her hobbies?

You may not know the answer to all these questions yet, but at least one of them should jog your memory of what the two of you have talked about. That's what you're going to use to ask her on a date.

A few examples, to show you what I mean here:

- "So, I was wondering: how would you like to try out that new Thai restaurant in town with me this weekend?"

- "I was planning to go to the opening of a new exhibit at the art gallery next Monday. Would you be interested in coming along with me?"

- "How would you feel about teaching these clumsy feet of mine to ice skate this weekend?"

- "I've always wanted to try that karaoke bar you were talking about earlier. How do you fancy taking me there one evening next week?"

The more personally tailored your suggestion, the better. Asking her if she'd like to "hang out" or "meet up" soon is pretty vague and doesn't imply that you've given this much thought – or that you've been listening. Asking her on a very specific date that you've clearly thought of in response to what she's told you is not only going to pique her interest (because you're asking her to do something she likes doing), most people are more open to a suggestion if they have a clear idea of exactly what that suggestion entails.

She's also going to find it incredibly flattering. It confirms for her that the connection she thought there might be between the two of you really is there. You like her enough to pay attention to what she likes and what she wants – that makes you a guy worth giving a change.

Now, be prepared at this point for her to turn you down because she isn't available on the evening you've suggested. Don't necessarily take that as a rejection – it's not time to back off and give up on her quite yet.

Instead, try an alternative. Say something like:

- "No problem – that play is on for two weeks. Maybe a different night?"

- "That's fine. How about a different evening, maybe next week?"

- "That's ok, we can always catch Adele the next time she tours. Maybe we could meet for dinner at the weekend instead?"

If she turns you down a second time, it may be time to say your goodbyes and leave – but it's much more likely that she'll happily agree, or make a third suggestion of her own. Bingo, you've got her date – now you just need to ask if you can have her phone number so you can call to make your plans.

And there you have it, success. You've taken this right through from strangers across a crowded room to blooming romance in the making. That's quite the achievement, so you'll no doubt be feeling really pumped.

One last thing: time to say goodbye. Leave her wanting just that little bit more of you and excited about the possibilities of what might happen on that date. Feel free to kiss her on the cheek if you feel that's appropriate or touch her on the arm as you say goodbye – nothing that's too forward, but just enough to remind her that you're interested in her to keep her thinking of you till you meet again.

Last Thoughts

If you've already been out there putting the advice in this book to use, I don't need to tell you what a difference it makes to your chances of landing a date with Mrs. Right.

If, on the other hand, you read right through to these last pages before you got started, then all that's left to do is put your best shirt on and head out into the big, wide world.

Things might not go exactly to plan the first time, but that's ok – we all have to start somewhere. The best athletes, musicians, scientists and scholars didn't get that way just by deciding they wanted to be the best in their field.

The very last lesson I want to share with you is this reminder of what we talked about right at the beginning of this book: don't be afraid of rejection. There's no such thing as a 100 percent success rate in the dating game, it just isn't ever going to happen. You aren't attracted to every single woman you meet, and not every single woman you meet is going to be attracted to you.

That's just simple math: every human being has different tastes and will be attracted to a different subset of people. If you don't happen to fall into that subset for a woman you've decided to approach, it's no big deal.

It doesn't say anything negative about you that you don't have facial hair or that you aren't wearing hipster clothes. It doesn't make you any less of a man, it just means you are DIFFERENT to what she is looking for. Let me repeat that: you're NOT "not good enough". You just don't fit that particular woman's list of requirements.

It's natural to be put off by the idea of rejection, but letting it stop you from getting out there and starting the search for your next amazing date would be foolish. Instead, I want you to accept that it's probably going to happen a few times along the way.

As the old saying goes, when it does happen you just need to get back on the horse and keep riding. Ask yourself if you can learn anything from the approach and think of it as practice for the encounter that's going to get you everything you ever wanted.

Because that approach is going to happen, sooner or later. You're going to see the woman of your dreams across a crowded room. Maybe you know right away that she's special, maybe she just catches your eye. Either way, thanks to everything you've learned in this book, you're going to approach her and kick off a conversation.

You're going to find out she's everything you've been looking for in a woman. You're going to connect so well that you'll forget there was ever a time you didn't know each other. She's going to say yes without a second of hesitation when you suggest a date. And maybe, just maybe, she'll be the girlfriend of a lifetime you've been waiting for.

Made in the USA
Middletown, DE
31 December 2017